Bug Soup
for Low Brass Duo

Seth Gamba

LudwigMasters
PUBLICATIONS

About the Music

The pieces in this collection were first conceived and written to fill a gap in the chamber music repertoire for the string bass. When I started working on these pieces with my students, the band teacher at my school was interested and told me that he also didn't have enough music for his low brass players. We reworked a couple of the pieces so he could use them, and the students loved them! With this experience in hand, I approached Clarence Barber at LudwigMasters about transcribing the whole collection for low brass.

These pieces have been carefully tailored to meet the skill needs of developing players and to harness the beauty and richness of low-register instruments. Students will sound rich and full without the muddiness that can come from simply transposing melodies and harmonies meant for higher register instruments.

These pieces work great for a teacher and student, a pair of students, or a whole group of students doubling or tripling the parts. If you and your students enjoy playing these pieces, be sure to check out the companion to this collection – *Vulcan's Forge* for low brass trio.

About the Composer

Seth Gamba is currently the orchestra director at Elkins Pointe Middle School in Fulton County, GA and the electric violinist in the rock band The Expats. He is well known as a composer and adjudicator having given presentations at the state and national level on topics including teaching rhythm, double bass pedagogy, and teaching class guitar. Mr. Gamba's orchestra has had featured performances at state conferences and his compositions have frequently been featured by groups performing at state and national conferences. His rhythm method book *Rhythms Projections: Rhythm Exercises for Building Mastery* is also available from Ludwig Masters Publications.

Seth Gamba grew up in Cobb County Georgia where he began playing the bass in the 6th grade public school orchestra. He earned his bachelor's degree from Indiana University with a double major in Double bass and Civics. He has a Master of Music Education degree from the University of Georgia.

Table of Contents

1. March Of The Crocodiles

Seth Gamba

Allegro

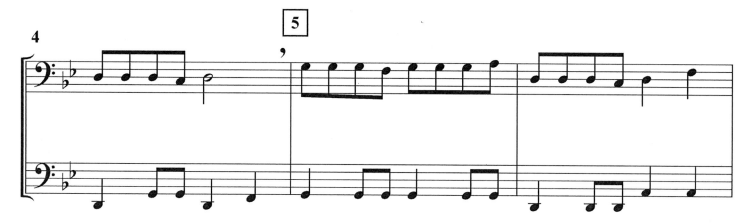

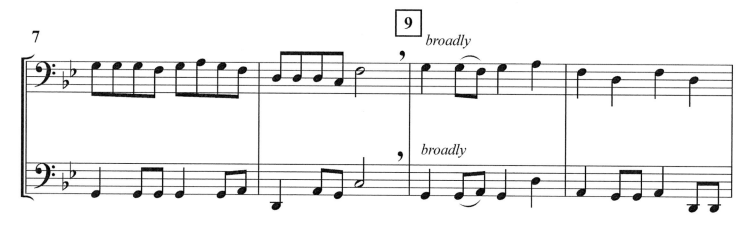

2. Warrior's Chant

Seth Gamba

Allegro moderato

Trombone/
Baritone

Trombone/
Baritone/
Tuba

5

9

13　　　　　　　　　　　**15**

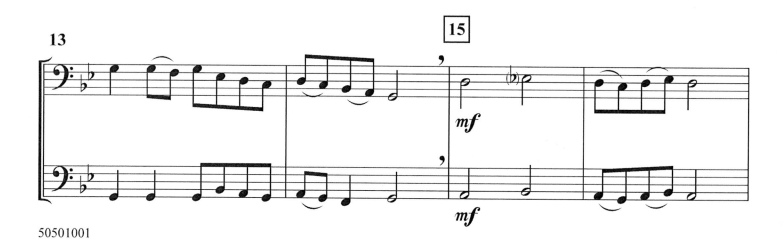

3. To The Sea!

Seth Gamba

4. Bug Soup

Seth Gamba

18

21

24

25

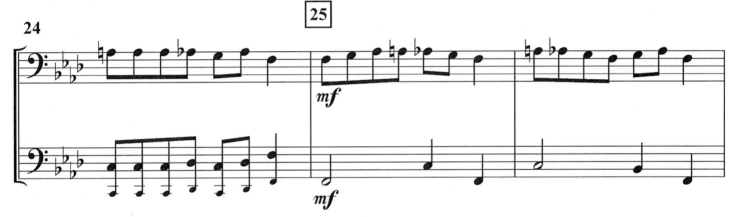

27

30

5. Walking The Dog

Seth Gamba

Moderato

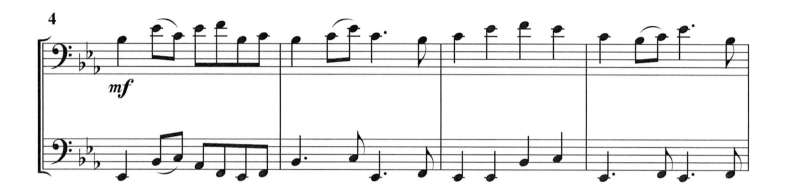

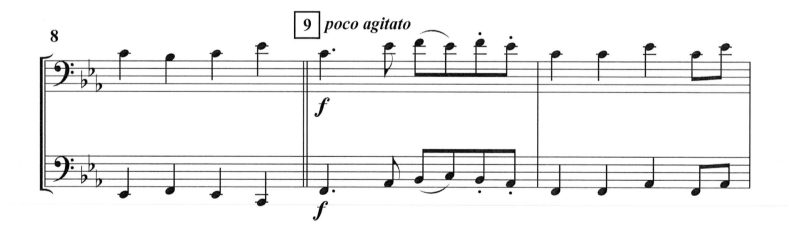

15

19 *relaxed*

mf

mf

22

25 *poco rit.*

6. Renaissance Fair

Seth Gamba

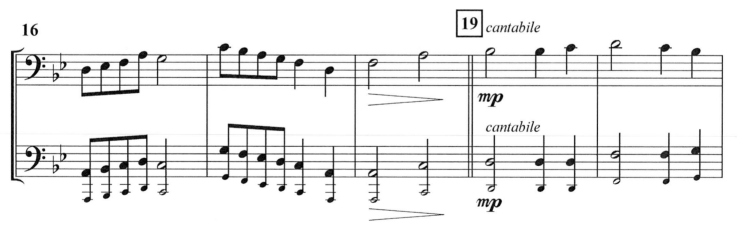

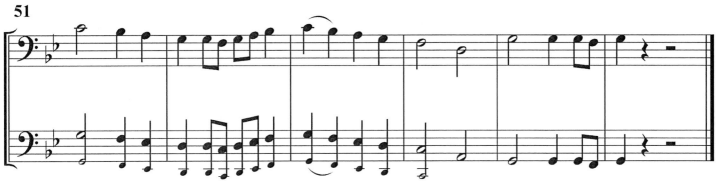

50501001

7. Sneaky Pete

Seth Gamba

50501001

8. Balancing Act

Seth Gamba

50501001

Selected Brass Duo & Ensemble Publications

DUO

HARRIS, FLOYD O.

10501146   Two Little Stars (Grade 2)

TRIO

HALL, PERCY

20502421   From Winter to Spring (Grade 1)

20502310   Regimental March and Canon (Grade 2)

The title of this trio is a play on words as the regimental march pictures soldiers marching and perhaps firing a canon. However, the canon is a canon in the musical sense. In this piece the three parts are marching along together to the same beat, but all are playing different melodies and rhythms making this a great exercise in independent counting and playing.The 8th notes must be short and crisp, but not chopped, and the quarter notes well separated. Baritone is a good substitute for the trombone, and the second trumpet part can be well played by a French horn with a high range only up to E. A tuba part is also supplied for the possibility of using the trio as a brass choir with multiple players on a part. The optional parts make this a very useful brass trio.

MOURET, JEAN JOSEPH

Hall, Percy

20502423   Rondeau (Grade 4)

NELHYBEL, VACLAV

20502309   Trio for Brass (Grade 5)

From the Festa di Discorsi Concertante, a challenging work in three movements using two trumpets and trombone. This is performance music, though a single movement could be used for contest.

ROSENHAUS, STEVEN

P002391   Triple Threat (Grade 3)

Here is a great way to start or end any concert! Triple T[h]reat for brass trio is one of an ongoing series of works written for trombonist and conductor Keith Johnston. This exciting one-movement work for trumpet, horn, and trombone is based on two basic ideas, the opening fanfare and a second, more melodic theme. Best of all, Triple T[h]reat is playable by pros and students alike!

TULL, FISHER

Stamp, Jack

50502001   Trio for Brass (Grade 4)

In print for the first time, this mixed brass trio (trumpet, horn, trombone) from 1967 shows Fisher Tull's genius as an orchestrator and his mature compositional style.

QUARTET

BEETHOVEN, LUDWIG VAN

Hall, Percy

20503214   Joyful Variations (Grade 3)

Joyful Variations is based on the familiar theme from Beethoven's Ninth Symphony which he composed when he was deaf. This arrangement begins with the tune presented as a hymn, and from there on Beethoven would not even recognize it even if he could hear! There are four variations in which the melodic line is the only constant and it is often quite distorted rhythmically. Variations 1 and 3 are in fast triple meter in the style of a jig and a tarantella. Variation 2 is in the tempo of a valse but treated as a canon. Variation 4 is marked marcato militant which ends the piece in the joyful style that Beethoven intended. The piece is quite challenging rhythmically and musically, but range is not a problem for any of the parts. This is an outstanding ensemble for use in concert, contest or church programs.

GARRETT, JAMES/ MORRIS, R. WINSTON

10503629   Wabash Cannonball (Grade 3)

HALL, PERCY

20503213   Fanafare and March (Grade 2)

MILFORD, GENE

20503228   Two Spirituals (Grade 1)

Options include baritone or F horn for trombone 1 and baritone for trombone 2. Both TC and BC parts are provided. All in F and all in 2/4, the first movement is lyrical and the second is a march tempo. Contest music for young students.

QUINTET

BRAHMS, JOHANNES

M323391   Five Songs

BURLEIGH, HARRY T.

M269791   Spirituals For Brass

CORRIGAN, BRUCE

50504001   Hoken Poppy's Gang (Grade 2)

GESUALDO, CARLO

Rager, Dan

20504212   Moro Lasso (Grade 4)

A somber piece from the sixteenth century about losing the will to live after the loss of a lover. A famous madrigal that makes a great quintet. Trumpet parts are in C.

GRAVES, PETER

M413091   Four Easter Hymns

Four Easter hymns for brass quintet, suitable for congregational participation. Titles include: Jesus Christ Is Risen Today; He Is Risen; That Easter Day With Joy Was Bright and Alleluia! The Strife Is Over.

ROBESON-HOWARD, MICHELE

50504003   Brass Quintets for all Occasions

These original and standard hymn tunes are perfect for weddings and other occassions. A wide variety of styles help maintain interest.

RYDEN, WILLIAM

M373991   Let Freedom Ring

STAMP, JACK

50504005   Suite for Brass Quintet: 1. Proclamation (Grade 4)

A suite of five pieces for brass quintet in varying styles, this work has something for nearly every occasion. The first movement is a rousing fanfare to announce its arrival.

50504006   Suite for Brass Quintet: 2. Elegy (Grade 4)

A suite of five pieces for brass quintet in varying styles, this work has something for nearly every occasion. The second movement is a moving tribute to Kevin Blair.

50504007   Suite for Brass Quintet: 3. Scherzo: Zack Attack (Grade 4)

A suite of five pieces for brass quintet in varying styles, this work has something for nearly every occasion. The tuba is featured in this spirited scherzo.

50504008   Suite for Brass Quintet: 4. Hymn: Let Us Break Br (Grade 4)

A suite of five pieces for brass quintet in varying styles, this work has something for nearly every occasion. A beautiful traditional hymn melody harmonized by Mr. Stamp comprises this fourth movement.

50504009   Suite for Brass Quintet: 5. Finale: The 10th Glas (Grade 4)

A suite of five pieces for brass quintet in varying styles, this work has something for nearly every occasion. This animated finale is a brilliant and satisfying conclusion.

WILLIS, RICHARD STORRS

Rager, Dan

20504249   It Came Upon A Midnight Clear (Grade 3)

Rager does it again! Here is a timeless holiday favorite that your high school students can play and sound just like the pros. Recorded by the Kingdom Brass Quintet on For Unto Us from Truemedia. With optional chimes and glockenspiel.

SEXTET

HALL, PERCY

20505192   Two Civil War Songs (Grade 3)

Many extra parts make this class 'C' work ideal for many uses. Very easy ranges for the young performer.

HANDEL, GEORGE FRIDERIC

Rager, Dan

20505222   Water Music Suite for Brass Sextet (Grade 3)

Three separate movements from the famous suite. Ranges are wide for all parts, but accessible to above average high school.